Acknowledgements

This book is dedicated to a wonderful host of people who have helped in so many ways.

To Dr. Jack and Mrs. Cindie Trieber: Thank you for allowing me to spend an entire week of writing from a campus apartment at Golden State Baptist College.

To Dr. Mike and Mrs. Angie Zachary: Thank you for the loan of study tools while I was working on this book, and thank you for your feedback.

To Mrs. Jennifer Palmer: Thank you for your excellent proofreading skills. Your feedback was also a carving tool throughout this project.

To my dear Mom, Mrs. Shirley Raynes: Thank you for agreeing to be one more "pair of eyes" by reading over the manuscript in the final stages.

To my Norman H. Taylor: Thank you for being willing to eat Parmesan Chicken again and again as my kitchen creativity took a back seat to writing.

To my Lord and Saviour, Jesus Christ: Thank You for saving my soul.

Introduction

Friendship is so often a misunderstood subject today. At some point along the way, the biblical concept of 'iron sharpening iron' (Prov. 27:17) has gotten lost in the fray of selfish motives, personal agendas and trophy companionships. The intent of friendship as a gift and a ministry has become more of a "what's in it for me" proposition.

God has a purpose for our friendships, and He often uses them as a gardener uses tools. Some friends are spades, helping to cultivate the soil of our lives so that we develop into "good ground" rather than rocky and barren. Others are like hoes, helping us to weed out problem areas. Still others are like watering cans, blessing us simply by encouraging and refreshing our souls.

In the 1828 *Webster's Dictionary*, you'll find this statement regarding friendship: "True friendship is a noble and virtuous attachment, springing from a pure source, a respect for worth or amiable qualities."

This dictionary notes that "false friendships" also exist, describing this type of relationship as a "temporary attachment springing from interest, and may change in a moment to enmity and rancor." If you've ever had the unfortunate experience of a friend suddenly becoming your foe, you know what it's like to have a false friendship.

A virtuous sister who is a faithful friend is a sister-friend.

Within every friendship, there is a bond of some type which varies from person to person. We may have many acquaintances in life, but as the saying goes, "True friendships, like diamonds, are precious and rare."

Biblical friendships are in short supply these days. We need more women who are willing to work at becoming all that God wants them to be, which will enable them to encourage others to become more productive for God as well. Living, breathing patterns of God's design. Sister-friends.

CHAPTER 1

Iron Sharpens Iron

"Iron sharpeneth iron; so a man sharpeneth the countenance of his friend."—Proverbs 27:17.

How would you counsel a friend who discovered her husband had been unfaithful? Are you the type of friend who would grieve with her and commit the situation to prayer and even fasting, or would you immediately push for a divorce without any further consideration of the circumstances?

What would you do if you found out your "best friend" had exposed a confidential matter by sharing it with another lady? Would you write that friend off as disloyal and shun her forever, or would you consider forgiving her for being too talkative?

These situations require the insight of someone who is spiritually sharp. When we lack wisdom and discretion, situations are viewed through the eyes of the world rather than through the lens of good judgment of Scripture. A woman who understands her vital place in God's plan will diligently work to cultivate a walk with God that radiates His presence and power in her life.

Iron sharpens iron. Proverbs 27:17 clearly indicates that God intended friendship to be used as a tool of improvement in our lives. A spiritually sharp friend is a positive influence, working in the Lord to help her friends become more mature in Christ, as they also do for her. A spiritually dull friend reduces the shine of Christ in the lives of others as she influences them with shallow values.

We get our finest "sharpening" from the Bible as the Lord 'transforms us by the renewing of our minds' (Romans 12:2). Undeniably, we cannot be the best type of friend if we are not spending time in the Word of God. Just as a lack of a firm foundation makes a building unstable, we are not as beneficial as friends when we lack the foundational depth provided by the wisdom, knowledge and understanding of Scripture.

A spiritually sharp friend is a positive influence.

Nobody sets out to be a poor friend. Sometimes we just don't understand God's purpose in giving us the gift of friendship. This leads us to take friends for granted. How can we become as "iron" that aids in sharpening others?

1. Be a daily student of the Word of God. People who read and study God's Word develop the right mind-set and world-view. A spiritually sharp friend bases her decisions on God's point of view, rather than living according to the way the popular winds are blowing. The less time you spend in God's Word, the less strength you'll have as a Christian. A person who is living a spiritually starved life has little to offer, but she can do an incredible amount of harm due to lack of knowledge.

2. Apply yourself to developing a prayer life. Prayerlessness is directly related to poor insight and eyesight. How could we let a day go by without asking the Lord for His divine direction? Our prayer life is the place where we deepen our friendship with God. In addition to praying for others, a simple prayer to add to your list is this: "Open thou mine eyes, that I may behold wondrous things out of thy law" (Ps. 119:18).

3. Keep your opinions to a minimum, but maximize the principles of Scripture. Even though our opinions are important to us, without a chapter and verse to support them, they are not strong enough to stand alone. For instance, you may be of the opinion that adultery is an unpardonable sin; however, your opinion would not be able to be backed up with Scripture, because the Bible says adultery is a pardonable sin. When discussing important matters, stick to the Bible, and you'll provide direction rather than confusion.

4. Don't be a spectator when a friend is headed for a cliff! Speak up in a firm, loving manner when you see danger in the life of a friend. There are times when a person strays innocently off course. When the error is accidental, you are helping to avert a potential calamity, and your warning will likely be accepted with gratitude. On the other hand, people are not usually as receptive to your admonition if they are determined to venture into a hazardous zone. Warn them just the same, if for no other reason than to keep your conscience clean and your friendship pure before the Lord.

5. Be an honest friend, but remember number 3. Your friend may not always ask for counsel. When a friend seeks you out for counsel, know that solicited counsel *is* often heeded. When asked a question, be certain you fully comprehend what is being asked so as not to cause a misunderstanding with your response. "He that answereth a matter before he heareth it, it is folly and shame unto him" (Prov. 18:13). Once the question is understood, give a straightforward biblical answer. Be prepared for your friend to become defensive when you counsel. Gently remind your friend with these three words: *"You did ask."*

Are you an ironclad friend who is up to the task of helping someone else to grow in Christ by your example? If not, work on the things in your life that will sharpen you. If you are sharp, stay under the hand of the Master Sharpener, allowing Him to keep you that way. The best friends are spiritually sharp friends.

It costs to be a friend or to
have a friend. It not only
costs time, affection,
patience and love, but
sometimes one must
even lay down his life
for his friends.

—Anonymous

CHAPTER 2

A Friend Through Trials

"A friend loveth at all times, and a brother is born for adversity."—
Proverbs 17:17.

It has been said that you are either entering a trial, or you are in the midst of a trial, or you are exiting one for a season of rest. No matter where you are on the map of affliction, one thing is certain: we all go on this journey at some point in our lives.

Friends are invaluable during trials, adversity and affliction.

We are so schedule-oriented that it is tempting to try to control every aspect of life, including adversity. Like an air-traffic controller, we attempt to designate the runways for our problems! "Problem Number Four, please proceed to runway seven for takeoff; Problem Number Five, please hold your position."

In the journey of life, it is not possible to set a schedule for when we go through a trial or for how long it will last. You cannot whip out the day planner and say, "Dear Heavenly Father, I'd like this trial to be like clothes at the dry cleaners—in by 10:00 and out by 4:00."

Ups and downs are a purposeful and even beneficial part of the fabric of life. Like dark chocolate, with the bitter comes the sweet, and sometimes sadness and joy happen in the same day. A perfect example of this happened recently when within the same day we received news that a friend of ours had passed away from cancer, followed by news later in the day that another friend had delivered a healthy baby boy. Real life is just like that—bittersweet. Death and life happen in the same day. Friends who help us through the down times are essential.

Have you ever gotten involved in helping a friend, only to eventually find yourself deeply buried in the details of her trial, to the neglect of your own home and family? This is a good indication that you have crossed the line from helping to managing. Although we are to "bear...one another's burdens," we must be sure that we are maintaining a healthy balance.

There may be seasons when we are responding to a friend's "four-alarm-fire" type of calamity, but this does not give us permission to become a self-appointed firefighter for our friends! Being a good friend during difficult times takes wisdom and discernment. Learning how to be there without being "overly" there is a necessary skill to develop in

11

godly fellowship. We are not meant to be a replacement for the presence of God.

When I was recovering from hip replacement surgery, I loved how my church family handled my very slow and difficult recovery. In swift, short waves, friends delivered meals, had a quick word of prayer or stopped by simply to deliver a lovely potted plant or gift. Since my recuperation was just before Christmas, one dear couple even came over to put up the Christmas tree, fully decorating it while I slept in the recliner!

My pastor, Dr. David Clear, and his sweet wife Valerie visited me during a time when my spirit was particularly low. Pastor Clear reminded me that I was down but not out! In this life, I want to be an active participant at all times, not an observer "sitting on the bench." When the recuperation became complicated and lengthy, I was not prepared for the way it would affect me spiritually. Thank the Lord for friends during times when the skies seem perpetually cloudy!

The friends whom God has placed in my life wanted to encourage but not baby me. Even though the process of recovering from hip replacement surgery seemed difficult to me, it still only qualified for what the Bible calls "light affliction."

Allow me to share with you the lessons I learned from these wise friends who walked through this thorny patch with me. First, I learned that helping must be balanced with a good measure of reality. Not one person tried to coddle me. In fact, Pastor Clear had a firm tone to his voice when he reminded me *not* to keep my eyes on myself! I needed that tone of voice! If he had said, "Oh Francie, poor girl, is the big bad boogeyman of tribulation beating up on you?" I would have been tempted to increase the length of my pity party! The godly wisdom Pastor Clear gave me reminded me to shift my focus off myself and onto Christ and even onto others. It was good medicine.

Another thing I learned is that a short visit with a person going through a tough time is better than a long one. This should encourage you to go ahead and make that call or visit that you've been putting off. When the going gets tough for your friends, any form of assistance counts! My soul was aided by the short visits, but longer ones would have been too much for me. Most people who are going through difficulties need a combination of support and quiet, in well-timed doses. Effective ways to lend a hand to a friend in need are making a brief encouraging phone call, stopping by to pray or delivering a meal.

> *Knowing that someone is lifting your name before the throne of God during affliction is precious.*

Yet another good lesson was this: we can be an enormous blessing by sending a card reminding the friend we are on our knees praying for her. Knowing that someone is lifting your name before the throne of God during affliction is precious and meaningful. To know that you are on someone's prayer list banishes the negative thoughts the Enemy has us believing and reminds us we have not been forgotten by God or anyone

14

else. Put a card in the mail the next time you hear someone in your church family is going through a trial. This is a ministry that really matters!

Other Times of Trial

Recovery from a medical event is only one form of adversity. In life, there are many forms of affliction that can test and try us greatly. It is good for us to be alert to the changes in the lives of others, allowing us to pray for direction in how we should help.

A friend who has a loved one in a terminal illness requires a particularly tender and watchful eye, as this type of trial comes with the added burden of knowing the end of the journey will result in the loss of someone dear to her. One of the best ways to help in a case like this is to look for a need you can meet. During the end stages of disease, the caregiver often is so focused on providing care for the dying that she may stop taking care of herself. Perhaps you could help with some of her responsibilities; for instance, doing housework, buying a few groceries, or performing another small task that has fallen by the wayside. Ask permission before involving yourself; stepping in where help is not desired may cause you to be a burden rather than a blessing.

A sudden death in a friend's family is another traumatic form of adversity which requires wisdom and discretion. While we would love to rush in and wipe the tears away, it is best to approach it in a prudent and thoughtful manner. Although we want to show love for a friend in such urgent need, phone calls can be overwhelming in these instances. Once again, keep an eye on the friend and family members to look for a need that you can meet.

Pray, asking the Lord to guide you so you can be beneficial rather than an added burden. We don't want to add to the heavy load a friend is already carrying by expecting her to entertain us. Instead, focus earnestly on praying for the friend and her dear family. Many times a friend's presence is more beneficial weeks after the tragedy than on the day of a funeral when she is surrounded by hundreds of people. Without trying to "make things better," stay alert and be prepared to provide an ear and a shoulder. Only God can lift up those who are cast down. We are merely helpers.

Quality versus Quantity

There will be trials and adversity which we must go through by ourselves. Believe it or not, this is good for us, because it makes us more dependent on the Lord than on our friends. It's so easy to rely on someone with "skin on." However, friendship can be overbearing and would be better when given in measured amounts.

When making loaves of pumpkin bread, I use a measuring spoon for the spices. There are several spices which would be easy to overdo, causing the bread to have a harsh, overpowering taste rather than a wonderfully pleasant, mellow flavor.

Spending too much time with friends can be like too much nutmeg in the pumpkin bread—a bit overpowering and not as enjoyable. Allow some reasonable time and space between get-togethers with friends, aiming for balance.

Neglecting friendships can be like a loaf without spices—sweet but otherwise bland. Our daily duties can cause us to disregard our friendships. Some of my favorite sister-friend times take place a day before I'm scheduled to fly out and teach a ladies' conference. Rather than looking at the calendar and wondering how I can fit in the time, I just get out my imaginary shoehorn and make the date fit!

Friendship is worth the investment in time. No matter how busy we are, we still need friends, and our friends need us. Set aside some time on the calendar for some quality time with your friend, to have soup and salad together, go shopping or maybe just take a walk. While we don't want to spend too much time together, we also don't want to abandon the precious time of fellowship. Friendship is worth the investment of time.

When Something Is Wrong

Have you ever had a friend pull away from you, seemingly without a cause? You could look for a way to mend a broken friendship by asking this question: "Have I done something to offend you or hurt you in any way?" If the answer is "no," then you are forced to leave things alone until the friendship resumes. Keep in mind that sometimes a friend has personal matters she simply cannot share with you, and she needs to process them on her own.

Other times, the friend won't specify what we have done wrong, leaving us in the dark. Search your heart and see if you can recall any incident, words or other events that could have left a friend stinging. Usually we know when we've done something wrong, but occasionally we may commit a violation in the friendship without realizing it.

I can remember a time when I called a friend to tell her that Norman and I had a full schedule and were unable to attend her daughter's graduation open house but would be sending a gift instead. It was clear to me by the tone of her voice that I had hurt her feelings.

This dear friend wanted me to be there to share in her daughter's milestone. What I thought was a small matter was a big deal to her. Not wanting to disappoint our friend, Norman and I reconfigured our schedule and were able to attend the open house.

While we were there, I slipped into my friend's master bedroom and put a large box of gift-wrapped chocolates on top of her pillow. I knew she'd find it at the end of the day and realize her friend meant no harm. Chocolates cover a multitude of sins!

Being sensitive to the feelings of our friends is essential; without sensitivity and care, people are often unnecessarily hurt. If you sense a breach in a friendship, do what you can to mend it. If your friend is not interested in reconciling, give her space but continue to pray for her and her family, providing an opportunity for the friendship to return or even become stronger over time. There are times when things never get resolved; accept it, leave the matter with the Lord and move on.

Learning to Rejoice With and For Others

Weeping with those who weep is just one side of the coin. Remember that Proverbs 17:17 begins with the statement that "a friend loveth at all times," meaning that we also need to show our love by sharing in the joys in our friends' lives. Thank goodness there are ups as well as downs in friendship! Has something good happened to your friend? Rejoice with her! Too many times, we are looking at life from the wrong angle. Instead of being happy for others, we tend to become analytical, wondering why God didn't do something equally as good for us as well. What a waste of joy when we can't rejoice with others! It is a mark of

21

character and maturity to be genuinely happy for others when the Lord has blessed them.

"A friend loveth at all times…" Love your friends fully, no matter what happens.

CHAPTER 3

A Friend of Integrity

"The integrity of the upright shall guide them: but the perverseness of transgressors shall destroy them."
—Proverbs 11:3.

In this society of disposables, it is no surprise that people have come to view their relationships as items that can be dumped as well. It is now more common to hear of people recommending divorce than to hear of those giving counsel to hang in there and work at reconciliation. That's why it came as no surprise to me when a young bride called me one day and said, "I want out of my marriage."

It is not uncommon for newlyweds to experience some immediate tests of compatibility. While they may view their marriage as being "over," what is often needed is patience, time and counseling, as was the case with this young woman.

"You are still alive," I told her, stating the obvious. "Your covenant is until death do you part. As long as you are breathing, keep working. Now here's your assignment. I want you to go to I Peter 3:1-6 and read about living with your type of man."

I also advised her to beware of people who were encouraging her to break up.

"You mean, don't listen to them?" she asked.

"That's right," I said. "Do not take counsel from people who tell you to do the opposite of what the Word of God says."

State law may allow for a hasty breaking-up of a

marriage, but God's law does not. She was not the first to navigate these marital waters when things get tough, but she was seeking to do what was right and not go on her feelings alone. After we finished talking, she went back to work on her marriage. As of today, she is still working on being married to a complicated man.

Good friends don't lead their friends astray. Have you ever been on the receiving end of bad advice from someone you considered to be a friend? There are many ways a person can be led

Good friends don't lead their friends astray.

astray—from misleading information to total violation of Scripture. How can you tell if you have a friend with godly character? The test is a simple one: People of godly character will not give you counsel that is contrary to Scripture. Now, we have to allow for the fact that sometimes a friend may give incorrect instructions due to error or a lack of knowledge. A person who has known Christ as Savior for years should "by reason of use have their senses exercised to discern both good and evil" (Heb. 5:14).

God has given us excellent guides through His Word—pastors, other skilled Christian counselors and wise Christian friends. We see examples in Scripture where counselors were used to fit various situations in life. Likewise, Scripture also shows what can happen when unwise counsel is given and then followed.

One very tragic example of a person who took unwise counsel is King David's son, Amnon. In II Samuel 13, we see a distressing story of a young man who allowed a combination of lust and depraved counsel to lead him to a tragic outcome. "But Amnon had a friend, whose name was Jonadab" (II Sam. 13:3). Having a friend like Jonadab was like having a reptile for a companion.

The Bible tells us Amnon had a half-sister named Tamar, and "Amnon the son of David loved her." There are too many problems in this story to list; suffice it to say that this was a tangled, out-of-order family!

Allowing himself to become sick with lust, Amnon sought out justification when he confided in his "friend," Jonadab (who was also his cousin), that he 'loved Tamar.' In the same sentence, Amnon called her "my brother Absalom's sister." Note that he did not say "*my* sister," but "my brother Absa-lom's sister," indicating that he was not willing to acknowledge that Tamar was also *his* sister.

The problem with this illegitimate lust was compounded by the fact Amnon was under the influence of his immoral friend, Jonadab. Cousin Jonadab clearly had neither moral compass nor any problem providing advice to commit an assault. You cannot expect to draw good guidance from the well of a person whose heart is full of wickedness and deceit. Amnon cared more about satisfying his corrupt desire than watching out for the purity and well-being of his sister; therefore, he sought a friend's advice that would serve his purpose.

In the end of this sad story, Amnon chose to follow the incorrect counsel of this so-called friend, which tragically cost his sister's virginity and later, his own life.

Who has your ear when it comes to counsel? Is it a person who is skilled in the understanding of the Word? Taking the advice of a friend who uses her feelings rather than the Word of God as her guide could damage your life.

Look at a few things when considering counsel:

1. Look at the lifestyle of the counselor. The person who claims to be a Christian while living like the world may not provide consistent counseling, and you may get your "ears tickled" with what you *want* to hear rather than what you *need* to hear.

2. Take a very hard look at the counsel being given. If it is not biblical, then you need to find another counselor.

3. Godly peers of your own age group may be excellent counselors, but there is wisdom in

asking someone who is farther along in life than you. Many of my counselors are ten to twenty years older than I, giving me an opportunity to glean from their experience.

Integrity Is Vital to a Friendship

What kind of friend would you rather have? A friend who lets you fall headlong while she knowingly watches or one who would keep you from falling by warning you in advance? God values integrity; therefore we also should. Proverbs 11:3 tells us that "the integrity of the upright shall guide them."

Integrity is not as highly valued today as it should be. It's just so "out of style" to have standards and values that are Scriptural. How sad it is that we have the Bible full of directions on how to live, and yet people still choose to make up their own way and then fail. It's like having a million dollars in the bank, but choosing to live in poverty rather than going to the bank to make a withdrawal.

After evaluating your friendships, choose to spend time around those who have demonstrated a fear of the Lord and who are living by godly principles. If you have not been a godly friend, this is a good time for you to consider your ways. We will all give an account to God one day for the way we influenced the lives of others. Being the right kind of friend would include being a friend of integrity.

Be careful the environment
you choose, for it will shape
you; be careful the friends
you choose, for you will
become like them.

—W. Clement Stone

CHAPTER 4

Gracious Friendship

*"A gracious woman retaineth honour:
and strong men retain riches."*
—Proverbs 11:16.

A woman came up to me after a conference to thank me for a statement I made in
regard to health as it relates to body weight.
I had been pointing out the importance of
taking good care of ourselves, while reminding the ladies we will never all look alike. It
is easy to misjudge someone based on her

physical appearance, when in reality we have no idea how hard she may be working just to be where she is!

"Thank you for being so kind about how you worded it," she said. She then told me how a well-meaning friend had made some unkind comments about her weight. Often these types of remarks come from women who are insecure in their own lives and are looking around for someone else to pick apart and criticize. The habit of tearing others down gives a false sense of superiority. It is insensitive and unkind to make comments about physical appearance, but it is routinely done.

I did my best to encourage this dear lady, re-minding her that we need to have the proper perspective on these image issues. Our motives for taking good care of our one-and-only "soul carriage" may need examining. A grateful Christian is taking the best care of her designated equipment in order to serve God with more vigor, not merely to receive compliments and accolades for her trim figure.

A gracious woman would not make thoughtless observations about a person's physical appearance. A gracious woman is genuinely caring, gentle, pleasant and as precious as she is rare. Her beauty is not merely on the outside; it radiates from a life spent in the Word and prayer. Just as Moses had a "shine" to his face after spending time alone with God on Mount Sinai, a Christian lady who spends time with God has a particular shine to her countenance and a tender, compassionate manner about her.

Take a look at this Gracious Woman Checklist and see how you fare:

1. A gracious woman is kind. Friendly and understanding are attributes which make up a kind and gracious woman.

2. A gracious woman is considerate. A gracious woman considers the feelings of others before she speaks. She gives thought to how her words or actions might be perceived by others, being extra careful when handling a difficult situation.

This woman is thoughtful enough to remember birthdays and other special events in other people's lives.

3. A gracious woman is pleasant. She is enjoyable to be around, not obnoxious or disagreeable. A gracious woman works at 'ruling her spirit' (Prov. 16:32 and 25:28) so she can remain consistently calm even in the midst of strife. An even temper is one of the pleasing trademarks of the gracious woman.

4. A gracious woman is valuable. Our homes, ministries, and workplaces benefit from the presence of the gracious woman. She understands that life is not all about her, but rather, it is about being of assistance to others.

This type of woman is of great worth because she is in short supply. Due to her selflessness, a gracious woman is often honored and appreciated. Contrary to those who view life as a race to win only for themselves, a gracious woman goes through life earning the trust of many people because of her beloved nature and her desire to benefit others.

How did you fare with the checklist? Every woman has a "gracious-section" that needs improving. One of my favorite sayings is this: "Little powder, little paint; make a woman what she ain't." This is a funny little ditty, but it has some truth to it. We can paint on a face that isn't our wake-up one, but we can't paint on gracious Christian womanhood! We're either gracious or not!

Time in the Word is one of the easiest things to skip.

The desirable qualities of a gracious woman develop by spending time in the Word. I mention this important habit at every conference and write about it frequently because time in the Word is one of the easiest things to skip, resulting in shallow Christian living. When you are tempted to put off reading your Bible day after day, you are depriving yourself of knowledge of how to live. You simply cannot achieve godly gracious womanhood without directions from God!

Another indispensable aspect of the gracious

woman's life is prayer. Without prayer, we can't ask help for the need to walk in a way which would best glorify God. We need the Lord, and we need to speak to Him not only daily, but throughout the day! If you've been frustrated lately over day-to-day issues, perhaps your prayer life is lacking. Have you asked God about your struggle?

Finally, a gracious woman is polished by hearing the preaching of God's Word. We graduate from "hearer to doer" by soaking up the preaching of the Word and then applying it to our daily living. Church is not optional to the gracious woman.

Madison Baptist Church in Alabama has a tradition of honoring a godly woman each year at their annual Ladies' Array. A dear lady is selected and then surprised as she is invited to the platform during the conference to receive gifts and much praise. Of course, the ladies who are selected are those who would rather not be put "on a pedestal" in such a way, but this type of person is all the more deserving.

It is a blessing to watch as the "woman of the year" receives her accolades. One year, the woman receiving the award never raised her head to look out at the crowd of ladies. She was so humble and unassuming; it looked like she would have rather been anywhere but at the front of that auditorium having such a fuss made over her!

Another year, the honoree was the woman in charge of keeping the church clean. Her "handiwork" was visible all over the building, and yet this lady was content for years to operate behind the scenes. These unsung heroes are gracious ladies in action. *They are being honored for what they do and who they are for Christ.* The Lord is truly magnified by their quiet yet steadfast testimonies.

It is possible for us to be wonderful instruments of grace without ever receiving a single press clipping. Are you a godly, gracious woman? If you are, your life will glorify God in ways which you could never imagine. Why settle for fleeting praise when you can have lasting honor?

CHAPTER 5

The Power of Influence

"He that walketh with wise men shall be wise: but a companion of fools shall be destroyed."—Proverbs 13:20.

Definition of a "clique": "A close group of friends or coworkers with similar interests and goals, whom outsiders regard as excluding them." (Encarta Dictionary)

Many of us belong to "exclusive groups" without realizing it, because we are naturally attracted to those who have similar interests. Whether positive or negative, these groups have a built-in peer pressure that can be either beneficial or detrimental, requiring the obligation to be like-minded. Peer pressure is something we think only happens in the teen years, but in reality, it continues throughout life. Unless you are a loner, you are more than likely a part of a clique. The type of people to whom we are attracted tends to be an indicator of the type of person we are and where we are spiritually.

Do you attract people who can't wait to tell you the latest news about someone else? This could be an indicator that you may have problems with your own tongue.

Do critics consider you to be good company? Then perhaps you have the critic-attractive tendency to murmur or complain.

Are you harsh with people? If so, you will likely have sandpaper-type friends who think being harsh is a normal way to handle people.

We are patterns for our friends. What kind of pattern are you? If your pattern would not please the Lord, then it's time to examine yourself and make adjustments to your manner of living so you will be the right kind of pattern.

What kind of person makes a good companion? "I am a companion of all them that fear thee, and of them that keep thy precepts" (Ps. 119:63). This verse teaches us that some of the best friends are ones who care what God thinks about how they are living. They are reading their Bibles, investing time in a prayer life, and seeking to live what they are learning from the Word of God. People like this can't help but keep us spiritually sharp!

Never underestimate the power of influence. Friends who fear the Lord will treat friendship like a precious treasure. A friend who has very little regard for God will water down your reverence as well. Our human nature tends to seek to be understood, even if we're wrong. This is a flaw in our makeup which can lead us to develop friendships

43

so we can "vent" our problems without taking any corrective action.

Let's consider a fictitious lady named "Betsy" who has some very serious marital problems. Her marriage has reached a point where screaming matches are normal, complete with escalating episodes of "mild violence" in the form of pushing and shoving. Betsy is tired and a bit fearful of this relationship. She begins to share her problems with another lady at church while they work together in the church nursery.

Over time, Betsy is giving weekly updates on the decline of her marriage, never stopping to consider what these reports may be doing to her listening friend. When a person tells someone about a serious problem such as physical abuse, there is an enormous desire on the part of the listener to want to help before things become too dangerous. However, Betsy is not thinking about how her friend may react; she is focused on herself and her problems.

This is just a brief example of how friendship can go off course, which becomes "free, no strings attached" counseling leading nowhere. What is the point of sharing a problem if there is no desire for a solution? It is this kind of unproductive complaint-filing that leads to only temporary relief for the complainer, while providing massive frustration for the listener who now has this negative information stored in her mind.

Please don't do this to your friends. A serious problem needs prayer and then godly counsel. If you don't intend to work toward a solution, then do not share the problem.

Finding Understanding in the Right Places

It troubles me when I hear a Christian woman say, "My unsaved friends and co-workers understand me better than the people at my church." Unfortunately, this is becoming a more common statement often made by women who spend long hours with people who do not care about God or the Bible.

Although a person has to be extra-vigilant in secular workplaces, detrimental influences can even be found within Christian environments. We need to pay attention and stand firmly on our own convictions. Unless you are trying to fit in with godly people, it is never a good goal to try to "fit in."

Why would anyone who is a Christian spend leisure time with people who aren't interested in things that would make them more like Christ? Could it be we have become so determined to have friends that we're willing to accept them at any cost? This is a poor plan, but it is a great way to keep from spiritually growing.

Who are your friends, and how do they influence your thinking? *Companions are more than mere acquaintances; over time, a bit of their personalities naturally rubs off on us.* It is just as important for us as it is for teens to keep a watchful eye on whom we allow into our inner circle. We often have a wrong mentality about influence, pretending that it magically disappears after high school. Influence, including

46

peer pressure, exists all throughout life!

Our companions will have an enormous impact on our decisions and our direction in life. Select your friends wisely and carefully, being friendly toward all, but only choosing to be close friends with a few.

Be courteous to all,
but intimate with few.
—George Washington

CHAPTER 6

Beautifully Balanced

"He that is slow to wrath is of great understanding: but he that is hasty of spirit exalteth folly."

"He that is slow to anger is better than the mighty; and he that ruleth his spirit than he that taketh a city."

"He that hath no rule over his own spirit is like a city that is broken down, and without walls."—Proverbs 14:29; 16:32; 25:28.

Are you a hothead? Do you blow up over things? Are you a crybaby? Do you fall apart with little provocation? Are you a moody woman? Do people have to try to figure out when you're having a "good day"?

It is tough to live with unbalanced people. If you can relate to any of these questions, then you are in need of an emotional overhaul. Here are some things which may help you.

First, we all need to understand that even though we don't always feel "sweet and cheerful" every day, the Lord has still given us the ability to 'rule over our own spirits.' It's sort of like doing a manual override to a system error on the computer. If we want a different outcome, we have to make some adjustments!

Steady, stable friends can be such good examples in this area. We need to develop the pattern and practice of holding up under the force of affliction. Life is not a trouble-free work zone! If you are prone to having meltdowns over small matters in life, what will you do with a full-scale crisis? Proverbs 24:10 says "If thou faint in the day of adversity, thy strength is small." It is vital to develop the habit of being tough on oneself. Stand in front of the mirror; point your finger in your face and say, "Look here. I've had enough out of you. Straighten up and stop acting like a toddler!" Try it. You might just find yourself obeying the order!

We must ask the Lord to help us rely on His strength in times of crisis so that we'll have additional strength when we fall short. We never know the depth of grace until we are in a time of deep need. Plan in advance how to turn your heart and mind toward the Lord during times of catastrophe or sudden alarm. Then things in life will not catch you off guard.

Anger Management

Of all the phrases coined in the world's psychological dictionary, anger management sounds like an absurd contradiction. If you're struggling with anger, you're not managing well!

Have you ever had a floating sense of irritation, but couldn't put your finger on the root cause of it? This is an indication that you may be dealing with some unresolved conflict which could easily become full-blown bitterness. Get to the bottom of what it is that's bothering you, and then seek an opportunity to have a discussion with the person or persons involved to get things straightened out. People problems are common, but we don't need to pile them up into a mountain of lingering resentment.

Forgive and move on.

Sometimes it's not possible to have a discussion that leads to reconciliation, which leaves us with no choice but to forgive and move on. If you've been hurt by someone (and who hasn't?) then you've probably learned by now that it doesn't pay to keep replaying the offense in your mind. It will only fuel your anger and magnify the problem in your mind. How does that help you?

Real "anger management" comes when we are willing to communicate well, at the proper time and in the proper spirit. This includes a willingness to "let it go" if the other person is unwilling or unable to see their part in the problem. Staying angry will only harm you. Is anger worth destroying your health? Not at all.

Tip Her Over and Watch the Tears Pour Out

Extreme sensitivity is another emotion that needs controlling. Since life is made up of a series of imperfect days all strung together, we are bound to have disappointments along the way! If you are brought to tears because of life's difficult moments, you are going to be crying a lot!

This is not to say that we should never cry. I once heard tears referred to as "God's washing machine." We all need a good cry now and then! The problem comes when we are so hyper-sensitive that we can be reduced to tears in mere moments by the antics of others or by a sudden change in plans. This type of thin-skinned living is hard on everyone, including the one with the thin skin!

The Lord wants to help us to learn how to rule the unruly emotions, but we must be willing to go through some "University of Adversity" classes in order to learn how to be a bit stronger. We can be tender and still be tough, but we won't be tough enough if we're too tender!

Is This a Good Day?

I once had a refrigerator magnet with this question on it: "If you're not happy today, what day are you waiting for?" That magnet was on the fridge during the years when I had two in diapers and one in training pants. The infant and toddler years seemed twice as long as these fleeting days! Even though I love to hold babies now, back then holding, scolding, diapering and chasing babies and toddlers was my full-time existence! I'm sorry to say that there were many days when I allowed myself to be grumpy over small things.

Do people have to tiptoe around you because your countenance is signaling that it's a "bad day" in your world? Does your family have to ask "test questions" to gauge your mood for the moment? People should not have to sneak around us as if we were land mines about to blow!

It is a matter of perspective to have a "good day" during the course of what many would call a "bad day." "It could be worse" is a good reminder on a challenging day, because, after all, things *could* be worse! If it doesn't cheer you up to remind yourself of this simple truth, try remembering, "It is good for me that I have been afflicted; that I might learn thy statutes" (Ps. 119:71). We can settle into the knowledge that the time of trial may actually accomplish good things for us. God sees differently than we see, and He allows us to go through things that are demanding and even strenuous.

Learning to rule over our spirits is a mental and emotional form of exercise. The more we work at it, the stronger our "emotional muscles" become. There are enough quitters and folks throwing in the towel, so there is no need for anyone else to apply for those jobs. What we need are more women who are willing to apply themselves to developing the spiritual muscle that leads to spirit-filled control.

Tale-bearing emits a
threefold poison; it injures
the teller, the hearer and
the person concerning
whom the tale is told.

—Charles H. Spurgeon

CHAPTER 7

Living Joyfully

"A merry heart maketh a cheerful countenance: but by sorrow of the heart the spirit is broken."

"All the days of the afflicted are evil: but he that is of a merry heart hath a continual feast."

"A merry heart doeth good like a medicine: but a broken spirit drieth the bones."—Proverbs 15:13, 15; 17:22.

An old Barbie doll commercial included this phrase: *"She's fantastic. She's made of plastic."* Sometimes when I meet a woman who is hyper-bubbly, it makes me think of the Barbie song! I'm not advocating extreme giddiness or plastic, pasted-on smiles (nor am I endorsing Barbie), but there is a time and place for exhibiting the joy that naturally flows from what the Bible calls a "merry heart." In fact, three verses within the Book of Proverbs show us **the benefits of having a merry heart** and its importance to God.

1. The merry heart makes a "cheerful countenance" (Prov. 15:13). We are brighter and have a better testimony when we don't allow ourselves to remain stuck in a negative gear.

2. The merry heart provides a "continual feast." This indicates a steady supply of joy, which we can then use to minister to hurting hearts (Prov. 15:15). Feasts are meant to be shared.

3. The merry heart does us much good "like a medicine" (Prov. 17:22). Wow! This is a free pre-

scription drug, designed by God to improve our physical and emotional health.

In our sister-friend relationships, there will be times when one friend is down and the other is up. None of us can dwell in the sunshine on the mountaintop all the time. It rests on the merry-hearted friend to help lift up the spirits of the discouraged friend.

Some people have a tendency toward being merry-hearted, while others tend more towards the guarded and pessimistic personality. We need to respect the differences, but for those of us who enjoy the "continual feast" of the merry heart, we must be prepared to minister to the needs of others. **What are some ways that we can be helpful?**

1. Don't dwell on the negative by spending a great deal of time discussing it. Bad things happen in this life; people can be outrageously hurtful or mean, and sudden changes can occur that leave a person reeling. Acknowledge these things, but don't park the car at the curb marked "negative."

61

2. Help a friend to put things in proper perspective. Why do we think that we deserve a perfect life, free of trials or troubles? Who promised us such a thing? Surely not God! We sometimes need reminders that good gifts come from our Heavenly Father, but if He decides that we need a dose of thunder, lightning and rain, then we need to become willing to accept the storm.

3. Spread joy cautiously. It is a good habit to learn to read people as you are approaching them, checking their expression for clues of where they are within their soul at that moment. It is foolish to run up to a woman who has a sad look on her face and then slap her on the shoulder saying, "Cheer up, my sister!" When someone is down, approach her carefully.

Do you struggle with depression or a sense of deep despair? Perhaps these verses from Proverbs will drive you to figure out what's wrong and how it can be fixed. There are seasons in life when we're just not going to be joy-filled, cheerful creatures, but we should not dwell permanently in the dumps.

Considerations When Stuck in the Mud of Gloominess

1. Check your heart. Is there any unconfessed sin or an unforgiving spirit that you have been harboring? Confessing and forsaking things that are wrong in our lives lifts off a burden and leaves us feeling relieved.

2. Check your health. Sometimes, we have something wrong with us physically that is dragging us down emotionally. From chemical imbalances to hormones, women have a laundry list of things that can push us out of balance. When was the last time you went to the doctor?

3. Pray for direction. Sometimes we may examine ourselves and still not figure out what's wrong. That's when we need the Great Physician to come in and "search us" for things we may have missed. Psalm 139:23 says, "Search me, O God, and know

my heart: try me, and know my thoughts." God doesn't want us stuck in a cast-down, dejected mode. Our enemy, the Devil, would love to keep us trapped in a bleak pit of discouragement. Ask the Lord to help you, and then expect Him to answer. We do have a God that both hears and answers prayer!

If you have a merry heart, don't take it for granted. Life changes quickly, and a merry heart can become downcast in a moment. Accept the fact that life has ups and downs, and determine that you are going to learn to accept the contrasts.

If you have a
merry heart,
don't take it for
granted. Life
changes quickly.

CHAPTER 8

Tongue Control

"In the multitude of words there wanteth not sin: but he that refraineth his lips is wise."

"A froward man soweth strife: and a whisperer separateth chief friends."

"He that hath knowledge spareth his words: and a man of understanding is of an excellent spirit."—Proverbs 10:19; 16:28; 17:27.

My husband and I were visiting a couple who hadn't been in church for a while. The goal of the visit was twofold: to ask if there was anything wrong and to determine whether or not we could help.

Usually when people drift away from church, there is a reason. This case was no different. The wife had been offended by some things that had been said to her at church, and she wanted me to join her in being offended, so she made this startling statement: "Francie, there are some ladies at church that have said some bad things about you too. Do you want to know what they've said?"

Yikes!

"No, thank you. I'm better off never knowing!" I said, feeling like a person who had just dodged a bullet. What on earth would be the benefit in hearing these secondhand comments?

The tongue is described in Scripture as an "unruly evil, full of deadly poison" (Jas. 3:8). When I think of poison, I think of the little yellow box of mouse poison called d-CON that Norman places around the garage in strategic locations. He puts these open boxes of poison along the edges of the walls and near the base of the garage door, intending to lure pesky field mice into eating themselves to death. A little bit of poison does the job fast!

The unruly tongue is like d-CON: it lures the listener, and then poisons her. We may consider ourselves to be spiritual; however, if we can't control our tongues, we're in bad shape. It's like saying,

 *The unruly tongue lures the listener, and then poisons her.*

"Come here, Sister. You've got a piece of lint on your clothes." Meanwhile, you are walking around with a stream of toilet paper attached to the heel of your shoe!

A good friend chooses her words with great care. When we are careful with our words, we actually increase our ability to control other vulnerable areas of our lives as well. Practicing temperance in one area generally leads to increased discipline overall.

Talking Too Much

There's no doubt about it—the more that you talk, the more likely you are to talk yourself into trouble. That's one of the reasons why Proverbs 10:19 instructs us that self-restraint with words is wise. Some situations, such as working with ladies in the church nursery, going out to eat as a group, or fellowships that include lots of free time, are breeding grounds for wandering tongues. We need to be alert to the potential hazards in these situations and prepare our minds and conversations in advance so we won't fall into the gossip pit. Plan some good topics to discuss in advance. This will help in keeping your discussions on safe ground.

Being a "Whisperer"

A whisperer is a talebearer who has a goal of

sowing discord by saying harmful things and criti-
cizing others. These people do have evil motives,
devil-inspired tactics against which we need to be
on guard.

A common trap of the Enemy is turning fine
friends against one another. Whisperers can't stand
to see happy people, so they will use words to
drive apart people.

"Did you hear what she said about your children?"
said Mrs. Whisperer to Mrs. Sensitive. The next
thing you know, Mrs. Sensitive is so hurt over what
was reportedly said that she is ready to cut off the
friendship without even checking the facts!

Most whisperers take statements out of context
and give them a twist, turning an innocent sentence
into something that sounds very disturbing. This
is how a whisperer works; she aims to divide and
conquer.

Don't listen to people who are anxious to bring
you the latest bad report about others. Interrupt

the sentence before it is completed; then change the subject firmly. You will not win the whisperer as a friend, but you will keep your heart, mind and ears clean!

The Wisdom of Word Control

Have you ever wanted to run in the opposite direction because a "stalker talker" was approaching you and you didn't want to get snagged? Unfortunately, you have encountered a woman who has not yet learned the value of measuring her words.

There have been some inconclusive studies done that have been repeated in the media without being fully validated. These studies indicate that a woman talks at least twice as much as a man. After researching this on my own, I found the study to be nothing more than unsubstantiated claims, but people are still repeating the claim as if it were scientific fact.

Whether or not a woman uses 25,000 words a

day is far from the issue. The real question is this: do the words have any value? We need to be more economical with our words, using them like dollars from a bank account. Just as we don't want to be overdrawn in our checking account, we don't want to keep talking until there is nothing meaningful left to be said.

A wise friend uses her words as though they were limited in quantity. We really can cultivate a habit of listening more than we speak, which will bring us safety as well as allow us to glean from the knowledge of others.

The next time you are tempted to repeat a bad report or to say something critical about someone, ask yourself this question: "Do I really want to have a mouth full of d-CON?"

CHAPTER 9

Forgiving and Forgetting for Good

"The discretion of a man deferreth his anger; and it is his glory to pass over a transgression."—Proverbs 19:11.

P.O.A.T. is an acronym for "Pass Over a Transgression." I know how easy it is to be tempted to hold a grudge. As one pastor put it, "Life is tough, and people are mean." The only thing that he didn't add was "so get over it."

We tend to catalog wounds, making it easy to revisit them in our minds. This strange habit causes us a great deal of harm. We stay focused on how someone has hurt or offended us rather than healing and moving on. This process of revisiting offenses fertilizes the ground of our hearts for seeds of bitterness to sprout. Why do we press the "replay" button on bad memories, when God wants us to press "delete"?

Relationships can go wrong; friendships can go sour; people can say things that they can't take back. All of these leave gaping wounds in the heart of the hearer. If we were robots, we could be programmed never to harm one another. Unfortunately, we're not robots; we're people, and people can do some major damage. Whether it's intentional or accidental, we just have to face the fact that in this imperfect life, injuries happen. The only way to escape this is by living where there are no other people!

Friends need to be prepared to P.O.A.T. You can't

have a sinless, utterly perfect friendship, because friendship involves sinful people. Even the kindest, sweetest people have been known to offend someone once in a while. If we make up our minds in advance that we will never hold a grudge against anyone, we will be on safe ground when (not if) we are wronged by others.

Forgiveness is not optional, but many treat it as if it is. We tend to be more willing to forgive those for whom we have more love or affection, while being willing to cut off others at the knees. Is this how the Lord has treated us?

God has sternly warned us against being unforgiving in Matthew 6:15: "But if ye forgive not men their trespasses, neither will your Father forgive your trespasses." What is there that we don't understand about this passage of Scripture? It's as clear as can be: forgive or you won't be forgiven!

Knowing we would have a tendency to hold others to a higher standard than we hold ourselves, God called us on it in advance. Our sin nature is never more apparent than when we have been crossed by someone, allowing the true fiber of our being to shine through.

Can you forgive someone, no matter what they've done? Scripture requires it of us, and to do anything less is disobedience. List as many grievances against you as you'd like, but you'll never be without sin, so you'll never be in a position to "cast the first stone."

Keep your life simple by forgiving and forbearing one another. There are no perfect human beings walking this earth, so we are better off accepting the fact that on occasion we will be scarred, bumped or bruised by someone. The goal is to forgive sincerely and move on.

Don't you love being forgiven? If you do, then learn how to pass over a transgression.

He who does not
forgive others
burns before him
the bridge to
God's forgiveness.

—W. B. Knight

CHAPTER 10

Privacy, Please

"He that covereth a transgression
seeketh love; but he that repeateth a
matter separateth very friends."
—Proverbs 17:9.

The lyrics in an old song include this phrase: "You talk too much." Talking too much is a real problem, and even more so when the discussion is about someone else's personal problems. Is it possible for you to know something others may not know, and yet keep it to yourself? If so, you are as precious and rare as a diamond. If not, you talk too much, and your lips need a zipper.

Due to a lack of emphasis on moral fiber, people today lack the discipline necessary to keep their mouths shut. It's just so much pressure knowing something that someone else may not know! It takes character to keep confidential matters private.

Even though a friend may also be a trusted counselor, there are many areas which should be off-limits within the realm of friendship. Here are some things that should be kept private:

1. Things that someone else did to hurt you. Unless they are going to be part of the solution to the problem, do not tell it. By telling unrelated people the details of an offense, you bias the minds of these listeners, tempting them to take sides. Unless you are reporting a matter to an authority, others do not need to hear what someone else did to you.

82

2. Detailed information about problems with your children. While it is natural to seek counsel from other mothers in this arena, we have to be very careful to protect the privacy and testimony of our children. Imagine your children overhearing a conversation that you are having about them. Always avoid painting a bleak picture of their deeds. It is fine to seek counsel when dealing with a difficult training problem, but guard your child's privacy by not going into too much detail.

3. Marital problems. Unless the matter is not too personal, this is an area that should be reserved for counseling. For instance, I recently had a lady ask me how she could do a better job reverencing her husband, as the Scripture instructs us to do in Ephesians 5:33. That is not too personal; however, if she were to ask me about something related to the marriage bed that would be too personal for me to handle as a friend. A trusted counselor is a better choice in cases of serious personal matters.

4. Confidential matters. If someone has trusted you with private information, you are duty-bound to keep it confidential. Even if you haven't been asked to keep a matter quiet, exercise self-control and keep unannounced details to yourself. Think about it: would you want people who aren't even related to your situation debating it without full knowledge of the facts?

It's amazing how fast news travels these days, especially with the available electronic tools. My husband has often said that it is not the technology that sins; it's the user. The Internet is a case in point. The Internet doesn't gossip; users do when they spread information that was meant to be kept private. In fact, there are web sites that are called "forums" that truly should be labeled "halls of hearsay" or "shelters of slander"! What purpose does it serve for private tragedies and events of other people's lives to be debated and passed around by big chickens sitting in little rooms in front of glowing computer screens? The practice of spreading rumors via the Internet has passed the epidemic stage. It's pandemic!

Do you want to know what is worth repeating? Good news! If you have to say anything about anyone else, put them in the best possible light. We hear too many negative things about people these days. Let's not participate in this unfortunate practice. As the saying goes, "If you can't say anything good about someone, don't say anything at all."

Leave other people's transgressions alone. God will uncover what He wants to uncover. The role of revealing secrets is not our job. Our assignment is to engage in that which increases love and the "unity of the Spirit in the bond of peace" (Eph. 4:3).

Let's have some privacy, please.

We hear too many negative things about people these days.

CHAPTER 11

Friends With the Authorities

"He that loveth pureness of heart, for the grace of his lips the king shall be his friend."—Proverbs 22:11.

People in authority need friends. However, in these modern times, those in positions of leadership are finding it lonelier than ever. People have so little discretion, as evidenced by their readiness to repeat confidential matters.

To trust your thoughts with anyone other than a spouse is risky, because there is always the danger that the person befriending you does not have totally pure motives. What can you do?

Recognize that God still provides vital friendships in these situations, especially if the people involved allow God to give them the right companions. Be a friend and have friends, asking the Lord to give you particular wisdom and keen discernment in your choices. People whose lives show genuine evidence of fearing the Lord tend to be good and safe to have as friends. People who live a bit too close to "the edge" in life (carnal and worldly) are a bit more risky as associates. After all, we are often thought to be "birds of a feather" when we keep company with people.

How can you be a good friend to someone in authority? First of all, let God do the leading rather than pursuing the friendship yourself. It is suspicious at best and disturbing at worst when people try to insert themselves into another person's life uninvited.

Be friendly and beneficial by helping wherever and whenever you can, without being pushy.

Another way that you can be a friend to someone in authority is by being supportive of them. Never be among those who want to tear down leadership; people who don't seem to care whom they hurt are not living right for God. Pray for your leaders, supporting them even when others are bailing out. There are no want ads in the paper for disloyal followers or fair-weather friends!

What should you do if you are brought into the inner circle of people "at the top"? Consider it a place of ministry and treat it "as unto the Lord." You are not serving for your own benefit; you are a friend for the sake of others.

Beware of Familiarity

If people in authority have allowed you to be an insider, it doesn't mean that you can take special liberties. It is important to remember that leaders should be treated with respect and appropriate-ness. For instance, unless you are instructed to do so, it would be inappropriate for you to call your pastor by his first name, even if you went to school together.

My husband and I count several pastors, mis-sionaries and evangelists as our friends; however, we are careful to keep an appropriate decorum which we believe is suitable for interaction with men of God. Just because society has become "first-name-basis" casual doesn't mean that as Christians we should adopt their loose traditions. Honor your authorities with appropriate respect.

It is also hazardous for a woman to become too close to a man in authority, discussing things that are unrelated to the ministry or the job. Intimacy is first formed verbally, and is later consummated physically. Too many people are falling into the innocent-looking trap of becoming too close on the job. Avoid discussing personal matters by only talking about what relates to your business or ministry purpose. Occasionally, personal things overlap with work-related issues. At those junctures, use discernment, being careful about how much you share.

Those of us who strive to walk closely with the Lord will often find ourselves in some pretty "tall corn" for company. Instead of taking this for granted, consider it as an honorable and important prayer assignment. People in authority often did not choose their positions. They would agree with I Timothy 1:12: "And I thank Christ Jesus our Lord, who hath enabled me, for that he counted me faithful, putting me into the ministry." It is the Lord who does the placement within the ministry, which is a humbling reminder for all of us.

I have many pastors' wives for friends. I also have many friends among the church staff through-out the country. I also realize my responsibility is to pray for them. What good is a friend who doesn't pray? God places us in the lives of others for reasons we may never fully understand on this side of

Heaven. Make it a goal to be a beneficial friend, lifting their names up in prayer.

Finally, if you are a friend of someone in authority, be aware that almost all of your conversations with them are confidential. Friends never betray their trust. You are not the local reporter for your church. This should go without saying, but some people need refresher courses in the basics.

It doesn't have to be "lonely at the top," if we will seek to be friends who can be trusted and have pure motives. What is the purest motive? It is love for the Lord and for others.

Never be among
those who want
to tear down
leadership.

CHAPTER 12

Telling the Truth

"Faithful are the wounds of a friend; but the kisses of an enemy are deceitful."—Proverbs 27:6.

Every woman who chooses to commit adultery has a friend somewhere. Every woman who dresses provocatively has a friend somewhere. Every woman who lives carnally has a friend somewhere. Are you the kind of friend that sees something wrong, but looks the other way? How are you helping your friend, and what kind of friend are you?

It takes a great deal of "iron in the spine" to be the kind of friend that would be willing to warn when warning is needed. No one wants to be seen as a busybody or a meddler; however, when it comes to hazardous behavior, the silence of a friend does more harm than good. Which would you rather do: warn your friend that she is headed for a cliff, or be silent and meet her broken body at the bottom after she goes over the edge?

Women today are being bombarded with false messages, leading to defective decision-making and rampant discontentment. As friends, we need to be more spiritually sound than ever. When we are mute on a subject, it may be misinterpreted for either agreement or indifference. Once a person takes the first step down a wrong path, the absence of input from godly friends may be misinterpreted as approval.

Are you wondering how you could help a friend

who is approaching the "edge of a cliff" in life? Here are a few suggestions.

First, schedule a time to talk privately. The church lobby is a poor counseling room, making it difficult, if not impossible, to discuss serious matters if there are other people around. Instead, try meeting in a neutral location such as the local coffee shop. Don't order food or dessert. This is not that kind of coffee date.

Another thing that you could do is arrange to meet your friend at her house. This may put you at a disadvantage if your friend is moving rapidly in the wrong direction, since you are meeting on "her turf." Your own home would be better, as long as the atmosphere in your home is beneficial and fairly free of distractions; children interrupting every few minutes would not make a favorable setting.

A last resort would be a phone call, which is not as effective as meeting in person when you are discussing subjects of a serious nature. Although a face-to-face conversation would be better, if you sense you are running out of time, make the call. Be sure to remember to ask if it is an appropriate time to talk.

Prayer is essential in approaching a friend who has ventured down a path that could destroy her life and the lives of others. Remember that you are walking into a minefield, and you need the Lord to show you how to navigate! Attempting to have a crucial conversation without God's direction could either make matters worse, or you could end up being cut off by the friend in need.

> *Without the Word of God, anything you say may be waved off.*

Once you have prayed about the matter and your approach, take the time to prepare a list of Scripture verses to apply to the situation, emphasizing the hazards ahead if your friend continues on this collision course. Without the Word of God, anything that you say may be waved off as merely your opinion. Opinions do have influence, especially when they are based upon Scripture, but why rely on something other than the power of the Word of God? You are employing the power of God's Word when you show your friend that she is headed for trouble and why, making it sure with chapter and verse. She can choose to agree or disagree with God. You are not responsible for what your friend does with the truth; you are just the "delivery girl."

To a meeting like this, bring your Bible, as well as a small notebook with a few simple points jotted down. To such an important meeting, leave your expectations at home, especially if you have not been asked for counsel. To paraphrase a saying, "Unsolicited advice is often unappreciated and rarely heeded."

Begin with prayer; then don't waste precious minutes on small talk at this urgent meeting. In trying to ease into the matter, you may run out of time or get interrupted if you're discussing the fantastic bargain that you got on a pair of shoes or some other unrelated topic. Just like approaching the ocean for a swim, it is best not to spend too much time tiptoeing into the water. Make a run for it and dive in!

As you are talking, watch your friend's eyes and countenance to discern whether she is in the "receiver mode" or not. If her countenance darkens and a smile becomes a frown, pause and allow your friend to tell you what she's thinking. Don't assume that you know. Let *her* tell you.

If your friend has a cosmic explosion because you dared to bring up a delicate subject for reproof, then move directly to Scripture, but limit yourself to a few verses, based on her reception. You cannot force-feed a person who has her mouth clamped shut! Do not try to force your friend to listen to reason if she is not ready to do so. Remind her that "a friend loveth at all times," so you'll be there for her if or when she is ready to talk.

If you have an agreeable response, continue to

present the case to your friend line upon line, precept upon precept. Don't back up the truck and dump the whole load, but cover as much ground as time and receptiveness will permit. Then schedule a follow-up visit to help your friend as she navigates her way out of jeopardy. Realize you may be needed for ongoing support and accountability, depending on the situation.

Our pastor often asks this question before getting into a serious counseling session: "Would you like the shot or the sugar pill?" These are truly perilous times, and people are drifting into waywardness more than ever before. To be good and godly friends, we need to be honest and truthful. If our friends are willing to take it, we need to be prepared to give "the shot" from Scripture, delivering it with love and genuine compassion.

CHAPTER 13

Tending Your Friendship Garden

"Thine own friend, and thy father's friend, forsake not; neither go into thy brother's house in the day of thy calamity: for better is a neighbour that is near than a brother far off."
—Proverbs 27:10.

I love the gift of friendship, but I don't get to see my friends just anytime I please.

Planning a get-together takes time, calendar-matching and other efforts! I have soup-and-salad dates on an average of once per quarter with a variety of dear sister-friends, but it's rarely the same friends twice in a row. Every date with a friend is a precious treasure.

Friendship requires some tending, just like a garden.

How often are you able to get together with your friends? If you are not able to spend a lot of time together, it may actually be better than too much time together. There is a bit of truth to the old saying, "Familiarity breeds contempt." In fact, Proverbs 25:17 says this: "Withdraw thy foot from thy neighbour's house; lest he be weary of thee, and so hate thee."

Friendship requires some tending, just like a garden, but we have to be sure that it's the right kind of maintenance. There are several ways that you could accomplish this mission (and feel free to think of some ideas of your own)!

Have a Coffee Date

My motto is "no java, no hava good day." I love a cup of coffee, especially when it's shared with friends!

There is so much that can be discussed over a cup of coffee. Recently at a coffee shop in our neighborhood, several ladies from our couples' Sunday school class got together. We each ordered our favorite beverage; then we ordered an entire platter of mixed bakery items! We cut the items into bite-sized pieces and passed the platter around the table. It was extremely fun!

Mixed in with all this sampling was a generous dose of questions and answers. Since everyone in the group had young children in their home except me, the ladies had many things to discuss. We used this time to cover some good parenting principles and to encourage a few hearts while we were at it. All this took place in the span of two hours in a coffee shop.

105

Do you have a couple of hours to spare once in a while? I have found that regardless of how tremendously busy I am, there is still an importance to booking dates with sister-friends. If we're going to help keep each other spiritually sharp and on track, we need to be willing to invest some time in purposeful fellowship.

Have "Phone Coffee"

"Phone coffee" dates are an excellent way to touch base and show that you care. One of the best days to do such a thing is when *you* are down. Why? Because when we take our minds off ourselves and think of others, it raises our own spirits. You can never seek to be a blessing to someone else without having some of that blessing backsplash onto you!

Phone conversations need time limits in order to keep them from running long, but the purpose can be to listen to a need or to call and say, "I was praying for you today." I call this "phone coffee," because it's almost like going out for coffee, only you are getting together by phone.

Keep these conversations positive. Murmuring and complaining by phone will leave both the caller and the called discouraged in heart and spirit. The goal is to be a blessing and to show that you care. Many people are hurting today, and with just one well-timed phone call, we may never know this side of Heaven how much that call may have kept a person from spiraling into despair or worse.

Home Fellowships

Hospitality is a great way to cultivate and broaden friendships. It also allows you to use your home to be an extension of the church as a "ministry center."

Norman and I invited a newly-saved couple over for an impromptu lunch one Sunday afternoon after church. It was a spontaneous celebration, and sometimes these are the best! This lady had just gotten baptized after being saved the previous month, and her boyfriend had trusted Christ as Saviour at the end of the morning service. This was certainly a joyous day, but to top it all off, it was also my birthday!

My house was not in "showroom" condition. There was wrapping paper on the floor in the living room from the previous night's family birthday party, and the gifts were stacked on the furniture. This happy residue didn't stop us from saying, "Come on over for lunch"! We had had take-out food the previous night for the birthday party, which meant we had a sparse collection of leftovers, a good head of romaine lettuce, some green onions, salad dressing and some deli meats and cheeses.

Party time!

While I made the fresh salad and sandwiches, we laughed and talked and got to know one another. The seeds of friendship were planted that afternoon, and it didn't require a big spread or museum-quality housecleaning in advance. It's not necessary to miss out on fellowship because we're aiming for some lofty sinless perfection in our homes or menus before we're willing to say, "Come on over." Don't put off building friendships because of some self-inflicted standard that isn't required! Take a paper towel, run some Windex over the bathroom mirror and have people over!

Don't put off building friendships.

Restaurant Dates

I love restaurant dates, because all you have to make is reservations, and sometimes you don't even need to do that! Some of my most enjoyable times with friends are when we go out on double-dates with our husbands. Now, if you're married to the quiet type, he may not be the one to suggest this, but if he doesn't mind, go ahead and get it scheduled!

Norman and I have the blessing of many dear friends in our church family at First Baptist Church of Rosemount, Minnesota. We are particularly blessed to have new and developing friendships

109

with the couples in our Sunday school class. Going out to dinner with just one couple provides a chance to get to know one another better, while going out with a group provides additional fun and laughter, causing some couples to form new friendships with people they had not known before.

On a double-date, it's best not to get into very serious conversations during dinner. I have never enjoyed a meal while discussing something sad or heavy. Save those discussions for meeting in your home over coffee or tea, or for a separate time of counseling. If a serious matter does come up, shift it to the after-dinner discussion time by saying something like, "We have a law. Nothing gets discussed during a meal that may interfere with digestion!" Of course, you would want to say something like this with a smile and in a light-hearted way, but it is true that food and serious discussion do not go well together. It's not that the food is more important than the people or their problems; you're just trying to keep the purpose of the date on track. If it's for fun and fellowship, keep it cheerful. When it's for counsel, leave out the food to better focus on the matter at hand.

Bargain-hunting Dates

Shopping is an Olympic sport for some women, but I'm not talking about that kind of shopping. I'm suggesting that you go shopping with a friend to combine two projects into one. Since getting together with friends is often tough to do, try combining it with a compatible project such as shopping with a purpose. Finding good-quality, classic clothing can sometimes be a chore. Taking a friend along on these shopping trips provides fellowship and an extra pair of eyes to critique the clothing choices. Some of us need friends to tell us to quit choosing every garment in navy or black!

You can have this fun and friendly time with just one person, or you can load a van and make it a grown-up field trip! An excursion to the outlet mall is a great time of fellowship, especially if the trip requires a lengthy drive.

111

Soul Winning With a Sister

Going out on a soul-winning visit with a sister is a bond-forming blessing. On a call one night at the end of winter, I had the joy of going soul winning with Nadia, one of my former mentoring students. She is one of the best soul-winning partners a person could ever have, as Nadia has a way with children of all ages, coupled with a sweet spirit.

Our son, Austen, who is the Soul Winning Director at our church, gave me the name and address of a young mom from one of our bus routes. He wanted us to visit her because this mom was struggling and was very discouraged. After a couple of tries, we finally got an appointment to go see this lady.

During our visit, Nadia had her hands full with four children, ages five to thirteen! At one point, while I was sharing the Gospel with this dear mom, my words were interrupted by what sounded like the loud honk of a goose! I jumped, and then turned around to see the eleven-year-old daughter honking away on her saxophone! It was hilarious, and added a merry note to our evening. By the end of our time together, that mom had trusted Christ as her Saviour and was beaming with the newfound joy of the Lord.

On our way to and from that appointment, the driving time allowed me to be Nadia's sounding board. As a young woman headed toward the wedding altar in just a few months, she had a lot on her mind!

Going soul winning with sister-friends gives you a very precious bond as you cherish the treasured memories of seeing souls won to Christ. You may even get a saxophone concert thrown in while you're at it!

Craft and Cookie Exchanges

Every November for ten years, I held a craft and cookie exchange fellowship in our home. It grew from about fifteen ladies the first year to about fifty at its peak! Although we live in a modest-sized home (not designed to hold parties for fifty), the fellowship was open to any adult lady. We had devotions at the beginning, then games afterwards. Dedicated crafters worked the entire time, and, of course, there was lots of food.

The very relaxed yet whirlwind evening would start at 7:00 p.m. and end around 10:00 p.m. Ladies would visit with old friends and make new friends. At the end of the fellowship, friends went home with containers filled with homemade treats and hearts filled with the delight that comes from spending time with good friends. It always amazed me how quickly the hours would pass, but I knew that we had provided a way for ladies to spend some quality time together.

How does your friendship garden grow? It grows by tending. Don't neglect your friendships. They are too precious and far too rare.

How does your
friendship garden
grow? It grows
by tending.

CHAPTER 14

Christ as Our Friendship Pattern

"A man that hath friends must shew himself friendly: and there is a friend that sticketh closer than a brother."
—Proverbs 18:24.

"Greater love hath no man than this, that a man lay down his life for his friends."—John 15:13.

Jesus Christ is the Ultimate Friend, the Model Friend. He loved us so much that He sacrificed His very life for us. What a sacrifice, and what a Friend!

When our friendships are patterned after this form found in Scripture, we find that our friendships have true value and deep meaning. When was the last time you slowed your life down enough to spend time learning at the feet of the Master?

We become better friends as we spend time with the Creator of friendship. There is no substitute for time spent with Christ and in His Word.

This is a great time to set this book aside and go and spend some time with the dearest and truest Friend you will ever have in life. In order to be a great friend, we must each have Christ as our example. No other pattern will do.

May God bless you as you purpose to be a Christlike sister-friend.